life is simpler towards evening

RALPH WRIGHT, O.S.B.

life is simpler towards evening

THE GOLDEN QUILL PRESS
Publishers

Francestown   New Hampshire

Library of Congress Catalog Card Number 82-84775

ISBN 0-8233-0359-4

Printed in the United States of America

"The glory of God is Man fully alive"

St. Irenaeus.

IN MEMORIAM

Edward John Hotchkiss	d.	22 October 1981
Nicholas John Clark	d.	18 March 1982

ACKNOWLEDGMENTS

I would like to acknowledge with gratitude the following magazines in which some of these poems originally appeared. In the United States: *Spirit & Life*; in the United Kingdom: *The Month* and *The Tablet*. I would also like to thank the Daughters of St. Paul for permission to include the poems "Woman," "Although Dust" and "The Father utters" which first appeared in a collection of my poems that they published entitled *Ripples of Stillness*. I am very grateful to Joan Yeagley, Austin Rennick, Kathy Dahm and Marcella Holloway for constant encouragement and helpful criticism.

CONTENTS

PROLOGUE

"It is the honourable characteristic of Poetry that its materials are to be found in every subject which can interest the human mind" — so read the opening lines of the 'Advertisement' or Prologue to the Lyrical Ballads of Coleridge and Wordsworth published in 1798. After describing the poems that the book contains as 'experimental' Wordsworth, writing anonymously, goes on to say: "It is desirable that readers should not suffer the solitary word 'Poetry,' a word of very disputed meaning, to stand in the way of their gratification; but that while they are perusing this book, they should ask themselves if it contains a natural delineation of human passions, human characters, and human incidents; and if the answer be favorable to the author's wishes, that they should consent to be pleased in spite of that most dreadful enemy of our pleasures, our own pre-established codes of decision." These poems, too, are offered for the pleasure of the reader whoever he or she may be. They are the product of the past 15 or 20 years of my life as a monk. It is considered more hazardous these days to put one's 'vision' into poetry: people immediately feel uneasy and talk of propaganda. But perhaps it is when we cease to try to share our deepest thoughts, feelings and beliefs — about God and love and sin and silence and violence and hatred and union and distance and time and eternity — that our poetry ceases to please or to inspire. I would like my poetry to be read and loved not only by poets but also by the non-poet clientele of our world. Men and women of every walk of life and every interest. From those who program computers or punch cash registers to those vice-presidents who make multi-million dollar deals and survey the world through the dark one-way windows of tall glass buildings. For we all have to cope on an almost daily basis with belief, unbelief, love, loyalty, betrayal, union, violence, pain, ecstasy, joy, depression, sickness, anger and death. The poems that follow are attempts to capture moments from these common experiences and to hold them up boldly and without shame for others to share. The Christian sees the dark side — sin, tragedy, separation, death. But he also sees the awesome beauty of all that God creates and the extraordinary dignity of Man re-created in Christ and called to share eternally in the intimate life of God. He already experiences in part the peace of his risen Lord and he believes that it is possible here and now to know in some measure the deep joy of union with God. He wants his faith to be reflected in his life and in his words for his deepest call is to give to others from his store — of life, of hope, of vision — whatever has been entrusted to him. If these poems are instances of this I hope they may succeed in communicating a little of this vision especially to those who, perhaps seeing almost nothing hopeful, may be on the verge of opting for despair.

life is simpler towards evening

PEOPLE WHISPER GOD TO ME

People whisper God to me
far more than mountains
for landscape beauty bores —
however roaring or majestic
is the pageant music
played behind
their massive faces
sunsets have no sympathy
and — for all its background
awe-inspiring paintwash —
granite cannot smile.

WOMAN

within her
and of her being
comes one to be
who will not cease

she speaks each day
God's Word made men
uttered again, again
and again
into our silence

hers is a dignity
that none may measure
hers a patience
refined by fire
hers a majesty
unperceived
in the painful tedium
of giving birth

the mystery
of her being
echoes the mystery
of God creating

and out of darkness
Light

SWALLOW

With a lightning dive and a
swoop
sweeping long and low
over rolling grass, hillside
and sudden pools
skimming the ground or the water and swinging
with boomerang motion
back and high in the air
handsome as Hector and sleek
as some Black Beauty
groomed stud stallion
— only for speed —
you knive your way
through empty air
with scimitar sureness
and finite ease
leaving a wake
of high peep notes
and with the passing
pen of your passage
writing beauty
alive in the sky

I AM A SHELL

I am a shell
listen to me
for the roar and silence
of the eternal sea.

A MEDITATION ON THE NEED FOR DARKNESS

somewhere a star was growing slowly old
in the uninfinite a light was dying
exchanging heat for cold and day for night
achieving a new darkness into which
sperm could be uttered to create a God

fire condensed to lava and became
through far millennia a cool dark earth
water and rock and air and even ice
were slowly there

leave room for the darkness, darling, leave me room
carry me, mother, carry me in your womb
towards eternity patiently into being

think what millennia did first gestate
with none, thank God, save God to count and wait
(who being eternal logically couldn't)
for all to happen

we are just one
one of a million million — how the mind
becomes so easily drunk with multiplicity
and reels accordingly —
one of a million million finite things
born of a burnt-out lump of coal
flung from the hearth of incandescent light
onto the cold floor of night
like a picked bone to a hungry pup

God too was born of darkness became Man
Christ needed like new grain the darkness too
to hit the earth and die in giving birth —
he was enwombed enfleshed and then emboned
undarknessed into being and embraced
there in the lamplit stable then not now —

leave room for the darkness, darling, leave me room
carry me, mother, carry me in your womb
towards eternity patiently into being

the awe would scorch our minds if we had not
gloved it in clumsy concepts to protect
us from explosion

he came but half an hour ago or less
in cosmomanic terms into our world
a world that once was light but had to be
a cold beacon of darkness to become
a womb unto its God

leave room for the darkness, darling, leave me room
carry me, mother, carry me in your womb
towards eternity patiently into being

the crumble moment of our frail words
ceilings against our heads

the cold star wombs the utterance of God
a universe prepares new silence
just for the possibility of sound

(and the Word was made Flesh)
the world achieves new darkness to leave room
for eyes to wonder at the fact of light
(and leave, it must be said, room for the blind)
the potter finds a way to fashion slime
from which might grow these hands
— both His and mine

leave room for the darkness, darling, leave me room
carry me, mother, carry me in your womb
towards eternity patiently into being

LUST

I lust
to be me
free
triumphant
unbound
by the limitation
of being
created

I lust
to be you
in a union
of ecstasy
where your whole body
and your mind
are mine

I lust
to be God
looking
with power
over all
from before
the beginning

I lust
to be me
to be you
to be God

but He
offers
all three

.

BECOMING MAN

The humble moment
of total fusion
in darkness
and silence
seen by no one
heard by no one
felt by no one
a greater detonation
than any nuclear fission
and for a long while yet
no one will know it has happened.

NAILS

It is the consequences
of our actions
that condemn
by their enormity
the moments of our weakness

each moment of blind folly
blazing
whether behind the wheel, the blade
or in the bed
begets
undreamt of sadness

taboos used
to keep, like barbed wire,
us from our lusts

now
taboos are gone
and we abuse
God's mercy

we claim the freedom
to make children
of fake love
and temporary union

we claim the freedom
to hire our minds

for a passing high
and, bored with being
merely human,
aim to be briefly gods

we authorize
a mother who
cannot forget
the babe she feeds
to kill her child
before she sees its face

and if a mother
is authorized
to kill her child
what's to stop me, brother,
kicking you
out of my womb

we have no care
for all that is and breathes
upon our planet
and are prepared
to blow it at one puff
all out of being

but God who once
watched his Son
nailed by man
and left to die
still watches and accepts
the consequences

26

of making man
able to love
and — when he fails —
even of making nails

When
God
made
you
there
was
silence
in
heaven
for
five
minutes.
Then
God
said:
"How come I never thought of that before?"

EYELIGHT

what makes eyes
that should be so a-
live with fire
blank and dead like
puddles of sludge
water on a
dim night
with never an even
neon light
to see by

or what makes eyes a-
blaze with vibrant
deepening light
sparkling with the
laughter of tu-
multuous mystery
filled with eager
welcome for the
one-time only
presence of a-
nother person

what makes men a-
ware that men are
relatively rare
a finite few
poised in a vast
darkened void

where even a billion
stars are only
pinpoints of light and
barely enough to see by

?

BIRTHDAY UTTERANCE

I have great joy
in knowing that you
have been
born
into the world
because
having been breathed
by God
into existence
you will never
be able
— like a bubble —
to pop
suddenly
back into nothingness

welcome
to this one great
champagne
dancing
party of being

and be
always
alive and utterly
grateful to Him
who
simply freely spontaneously
needlessly and
eternally
utters

31

PASCHALE
on the day of her baptism

Words fall gently like the dull
slow rain of the autumn day
grey with the mood of winter —
water flows bearing eternity
driftwood into time
while blindness lounges proudly against
the church windows —
tiredly we grope in broken prayer
faintly towards belief and hear
omnipotent Light
— for our new hope —
articulate a person,
poise in our brutal oyster world
a micro God-begotten pearl,
a trumpet note with a dying fall —
Paschale.

CHRISTINA
five months

with the eyes of Columbus
Christina caresses the rough
edge of the world
and with tiny fingers
watches with delicate wonder
touching exploring and stroking
all
with unmixed delight —
smiling and giggling she welcomes
the outstretched hands
that hold her gladly a moment
believing that all of creation
bends to be her perfection
and as she creates
a limited landscape
around her of smiles
finding it all
— all of it —
good

ALTHOUGH DUST

Although dust
I am loved
by the one
eternal
Son of the Father
just as intensely
as this same Father
loves his one
eternal Son

O mystery
O majesty
O wonder
that what we
in our wildest dreams
could not conceive
has been
by God's own Word
quietly revealed

REDWOODS SOAR

Redwoods soar
into their own silence
creating a calm richer
than the calm of graveyards
or of ruined abbeys
or even of pyramids —
their silence in the sunlight
is more intense
and their shadow
teaches the full mystery of light
conveying
the majesty of seasons and of change —
their utter stillness
makes a way
for measured movement —
in their light and darkness are displayed
endless patterns of beauty
at their feet and in their shade
grass waves carefully
throwing a casual shadow —
even insects find
in their silence and against
their darkness
their own bright place for being
poised or darting
like a scratch across a window pane
fast to another poise —
here
silence is sacred
I feel a need

to ask permission to breathe
speech seems almost sacrilegious
even thought seems out of place
and I am at ease
only with wonder —
shade from the tall
sundial trees
tells it is already
after noon and soon
only the tops of the tallest trees
will be able to tell
— for a little while longer —
the glory of sunlight

HAIKU?

God laughing
me into being
and you too —
a joke to remember.

FOR HUGH
aged eight

For Hugh
whose smile
makes everything worth while
and who
can plant a happiness where once
a sadness grew —
whose laughter and whose joy must ring
around the faces peering in —
and who
will tell you with the eyes of Eve
before she sinned that if you're brave
and bounce along through life and try
to learn quite hard and not to cry
too much —
that you'll be happy too
— sometimes —
for Hugh

CHILDHOOD

Why can't eternity start at ten
or nine and a half in the sunlight
with vigor and life and laughter
and surgings of joy
and bubblings of almost-still-innocence
why can't eternity start
let time stop
who wants to be
older
or wiser
or more disillusioned
but fools
come Lord stop the clock
break into with music
our premature longing
amber the
caught-in-a-moment-of-cobweb-sunshine
fly of our childhood
and keep us
in laughter and song
excitement and mystery
playfully searching and dancing
through woods of discovery
through all eternity too
wonderfully poised
towards you

I WILL WRITE OF MOMENTS

I will write of moments
tasted together — new wine —
to a background of confident
rhythmical stark 'griechische Musik'
untouched by dreams.
I will write in thanks
for the simple joy
of finding a friend
whom — if I were God —
I would have created.
I will write of what must remain
forever wordless
— thoughts
caught in the frail
net of the intellect —
for only the heart
really can tell
(but cannot being tongueless)
of what I am writing —
and writing now
before the snow falls
and the slow song of autumn
dies in the distance
and before this moment
is lost in the sunlight
the misted sunlight
of smouldering leaves —
and now I have said
almost nothing
and it is written.

HE TOLD THE TIME IN LIGHT YEARS

He told the time in light years
— they used to say —
watching the stars poised
against the night
telling that man was brief
sudden to fall
a shooting star rather than autumn leaf
small
drifting in vacuo —

he told the time in light years meaning that God
did more becoming Man than man can know
he told the time in light years to unblind
the mind of man unto the real calm
of simply being

                tired light
reaching across the distance without end
claiming it once was stars

they used to say
he told the time in light years to remind
himself and others who might care to ask
that time remains uttered by God for good
simply the toy of childhood

TIME

Time is God's vast
sense of humor
a rampant melodious
half-mysterious
semi-courteous
practical joke
on men microbes
rocks rhinos
thinkers and things
flung in an ordered
pattern of tight con-
tinuous moments
into being
a long queue
for Fish & Chips
waiting in line to be different.

Can you see
the vast joke
of suddenly being
and never the same?
Isn't this
an absurd game
for an Almighty
to want to play?
Yet if our reasoning minds refuse it
time still remains
— a clown might say —
God's chance of music.

OCCURRENCE

You might have been born in Hong Kong
when Ghengis Khan
was pounding the planet.
Or even today, aeons away,
in London or Tokyo.
But somehow someone's kindly computer
decided
that you should be
roughly here
roughly now
and with four thousand million
currently elsewhere
I almost explode
with thanksgiving
as I blunder
like some beautiful rhino
casually out of the bush
into the path of your being.

THE FEEL OF THE RAIN

This time I have barely a word
to launch you forth
into the wide bold world
that awaits you —
only the feel of the
wind and the rain and the sun
on your nose and your eyes
and a dim sense of peace in the presence
of someone whose eyes would say
"Be not afraid, I am with you
wherever you are —
I am with you to love you in sunlight,
to keep you in rain,
to guard you in lightning, thunder and darkness
and be with you always
— beyond all silence —
offering a life that will blend
with these few moments of time
into my life without end."

WESTON LODGE

Time is not gentle with a last goodbye —
the body changes while the mind
remembers and forgets the things
that yesterday were consciousness —
the house the trees the gravel of a home
cling like toffee to the fading wrapper
of fast years —
a home is more than just a place
to say goodbye to
but less than quite a person —
perhaps it is ourselves
younger and more innocent than now
to which we wave adieu —
childhood thrown up by the last spring tide
half-buried in the sand —
we turn reluctantly and slowly move
inland

WHEN I WRITE

when I write
of the joy
of life with God

I think of you
being
for that moment
one with me

then I wonder
why that moment
ever ended
and I long
for when it won't

A POEM FOR JUDY

reading your poems I am aware of wine
constrained in a cask within the dark
cellar of your heart

a wine won from a chosen vintage
— grapes that hung in full sunlight
until they were ripe for treading —

a wine mellowing through the years of silence
towards an appointed glory in the glass

NIGHT CROSSING

your quiet smile
and warm simplicity
as ripples of gold and amber light
measured the dark waters of Dunkirk
told me of a friendly God
and of eternity

life is torn with minor tragedies
of simple meetings broken by goodbye
— the little facts of time and space
that give to possibility
too much of being
and make of chance
a fool's hypothesis
against His silent unperceived
and yet incisive
Everywhere —
I knew of you only enough
to want to know more
but rather less than would let me
learn your address

as you climbed on the train I was left
holding your name
but with it a memory
that will remain
of the light within your eyes
making ripples of gold
and amber music

echo over the dark waters
of Dunkirk a good while
before dawn

WHEN MONIKA SMILES

When Monika smiles
sadness leaves her eyes
as twilight runs
from the spreading dawn
but before I may lie
and bask in her laughter
dusk falls with the calm
of the autumn leaf
for only joy
can bear the weight
of her inexpressible
infinite grief
and joy is brief.

THE SHADOW OF THE WIND

I have seen with you
the shadow of the wind
thrown by tall trees
guarding the dark water
the shadow of the wind
keeping a certain calm
against the constant turbulence
of changing light and darkness
I have seen in you and known
the shadow of the wind
as clouds race white and black
across the sky
and in this calm I found
a joy that cannot fear
what dark may do to me beyond
the shadow of the wind.

THE FATHER UTTERS

The Father utters
a Word
which a virgin
receives

the Spirit speaks
and the virgin who listens
utters
the Word

heard
once by the prophets
the Word now speaks
while the world listens

to the mercy and myriad
wonders the Father
utters

INCARNATION

Incarnation means that the
start of the world
was not just the slow
burst of a star
cooling through aeons
into the night
but rather a barely
conceivable moment
wombed on the darkened
rim of eternity
and costing God
— in giving birth —
His life.

MIDNIGHT ROBBERY

he came into the world half by surprise
a brick thrown by a robber
into a jeweller's window
while constellations and night watchmen
told of his coming which left
our gold devalued

priests strode
with heads high
watching half amused
the ignorant passers-by
tried their smiles before the glass at dawn
and wiped their words before and after use

burning through the ingots of the law
he made a way for unknown freedom
cutting with acetylene incision
through skin class and culture slaveries
laying bare that riches lie
in harboring an open heart
wide bold and poor enough
to welcome all
while breaking in a word
our prison bars
'Father'

he came spoke and having spoken
went
we broke his body for his stark abuse
of all we counted

he died with our desertion on his lips
between thieves
rending gold foundations

but gold crept back in trinkets
winking at the will
whispering mastery security
seclusion
bringing back a windowful
of mere jewels

if he came again tonight
out of the dark
shattering our iconostasis
robbing our complacency
in passing things
BBC would give him half an hour
but afterwards
would things be very different?

FRIEND

you will be my Simon through the years
bearing the burden of my loneliness
from Cyrene
climbing together
against the gravity of pride
our calvary
breaking our toes
against the daily rubble of our falls
and disappointment
you
through every joy and grief
passion or despair
from me
in this hour before eternity
may God never hide
or in his love
too lastingly or rendingly
divide

UNLESS A GRAIN

I am still stunned
at being
a grain
of wheat

dropping
in slow motion
into
the earth

at times almost leaping
but always longing
to watch and not be the explosion!

PASSION

There is huge danger
in sweet success
with its flammable vapor
of self conceit
for the greatest thing
we can ever do
is to let ourselves
receive his love
who flat on his back
against the wood
received our nails
to heal the world.

AS YOU PASSED BY ME

as you passed by me
lying
with nothing beautiful about me
helpless
caught in my sin
like a beast in a trap
you looked at me —
dark water with the distant stars
of deep love reflected
in all the calm of tenderness —
you didn't even have a chance to speak
they needed you elsewhere too quickly
but in your wake you left me
quickened into knowing
by that glance
my dignity in being loved by you

FOOL

Fool — I said to myself
why so proud of being
for such a brief
flash in the wide
pan of the universe
somebody — master of all —
standing and fronting the sun
but unable to be
for more than the sigh that it takes
to grow old —
Fool — I said — be your age
be intensely
be molten and rage
be loud be coloured be new
be open be air
be there
to breathe and be breathed
but be not deceived
be awake be aware
of your size and be proud
— if at all —
Fool be proud
be proud
to be small

SWAN

Slow
glide me over between
in the pride of your wake
deep dark
turbulent dark
marble moving
poplar reflecting
black
— almost canal-colored —
royal sweep curved
slanting back
intent to push so unla-
boriously forward and from
charcoal brows you
glory in orange and gold
the white-against-black
of being
so unsuspectedly
silently
regally
almost self-consciously
almost aware of and glad to be
no one but you
mute in your mastery
proud
so proud
to be seen

FALL BEAUTY

reflected in the window of the door
aslant against the midnight purple wall
the leaves outside are dancing in the wind
in yellow amber green and sudden gold

so great an exhibition of His work
in casual excess
is always hard to find
and yet

the claim is limited
that one brief leaf may have on our concern
while God
to whom we'd think we would appear as leaves
has proved the hold we have upon His heart
unlimited

IF DEATH

if death
is not
the doorway to life
then I
am just
a superior leaf
hanging a season
out of the sky
then falling briefly
into the earth
small manure
barely enough
to properly dung a rose with

ROSE

from folded bud
to open bloom
you move like royalty
knowing yourself adored

accepting from
the silence of the dawn
your sole applause
you move
from youth towards magnificence
while the proud mates
of potentates
for dignity
borrow your fragrance

your colors are
the arbiters of excellence
all bow
before your being

when the symphony is over
and you die
Eden is empty

TWO TREES

two trees
proclaim in spring
a word to the world

one exploding
into blossom
trumpets glory

one stretching
dead limbs
holds the empty
body of God

both speak
with due reserve
into the listening
ear of the world

PENTECOST

Like the whetted metal of meths*
words probe me
tongued with olympic torches that flame
throwing orange and lemon fire as I run
wild wild with the joy
of being
free of the lash and shackle of law
freed by the living power of the man
once
nailed to a tree — Christ —
writhing molten within me
moulded tamed gentle and calm
carefree yet tempered wild
wild with a joy
that leaves the darkness blazing behind me
and wreathes me in olive
wild to be now
unendingly although defiled
God's child.

* "Methylated spirits" or "meths" is ethyl alcohol denatured
with methyl alcohol for the purpose of preventing its use as an
alcoholic beverage. In Britain "meths" is drunk with devastat-
ing results by some alcoholics as the cheapest form of alcohol
available.

TRUNCATE

Redwood trees
have soared in silence
for thousands of years
along our shores
their age
their calm
their dignity
command respect

scions thrusting
from the roots of Jesse
across our land
towards eternity
are axed daily
without awe
out of being

PAIN
for Robert

The pain
pendulums back and forth
and still
restlessly
I do not understand
to and fro, to and fro
pulsating in my blood, my brain
like rains of dark blood
deepening this huge
great wound of night
the pain, the pain
leans hard against my brain
beats hard against
the windows of my dawn

                    my faith

                          my dreams

visions of what God calls to be
my hope
the pain the pain the pain
swings wide arms to and fro
gesticulating feverishly
against all chance of meaning while the blinds
— the blindness — has upon my mind
utterly descended
I do not under-
stand I do not, do not
understand I do not
understand the pain

that needles white-hot wires within
my brain takes all away
takes all away
takes all
away

only the looming beam upon the hill
against a storm-rent sky
brings mystery to my nonsense
and my pain
the claim that God once uttered
carefully casually at a point in time
his first-born Son into the human pageant
to feel the edge of man's fine hatred —
the claim that man
still blindly drunk on the age-old
vintage of his arrogance
nailed his God hard down against the wood
that God himself had uttered
and leaned him up for fun against the sky
in pain
to watch him die

the awesome mystery of these brief events
calms the loud nonsense raging in my mind
brings me to new dimensions of new awe
and helps me bear the pointlessness of pain
the rude mockery of his infinite goodness
without explosion

and yet the pain swings back
circles like vultures on Prometheus Bound
probes the recesses of each angry nerve
goads me from calm to tortured restlessness
breaking me down till I can offer God
the nothing nothing that I really am
a seething raw and aggravated being
stretching thin fingers constantly towards
the hand that utters

LEAF FALL

I was not watching but I heard
a leaf fall off an indoor plant just now
and hit the carpet in the perfect stillness —
as it fell it touched another leaf
and so I heard its fall —
there was no kind of wind or other force
to cause this brief event, it seems it fell
simply because it had been growing
silently old long enough
to earn this parting —
it may be at least a week or even a month
before another leaf from the same plant
merits this moment
so what a simple grace and gift it was,
and quite uncalled for,
to be there at this instant not to watch
— as one might watch a lift-off towards the moon —
but, as befits its call to be discreet,
only to hear the falling of this leaf.

APART

My falls are loneliness
reaching for comfort —
Eli, Eli,
why have you forsaken me? —
loneliness started
when I began —
at my conception I left
father and mother became
myself alone apart
from other matter
persons or things —
from the moment of leaving the dark
warmth of the womb
till when I become
cold flesh to be tipped
into the earth
life distils distance —
slowly I grow
towards the time
the fierce brief time
of union —
a time when we cling
together for warmth
against the arctic
of being alone —
after this moment
we turn and learn
to live with distance —
lama sabachthani —

falling years
draw us towards
the inconceivable —
but before we may find
the undreamt smile
we must become ugly
and undesired
and as the boat pulls farther
from the harbour walls
with the dark water deepening
cold between us
we must feel in our bones
the agony of distance
and learn in flesh
what being matter means —

DISTANCE GIVES THE MEN OF WAR THEIR HOLD

Distance gives the men of war their hold,
  kept to keep me capable of hate.
I cannot love the men I do not know
  and, lest I love, they keep between us space.

They character your person with black paint,
  feeding me a myth with subtle skill.
They keep me from the knowledge of your face
  — that I may kill.

Idea-logians smile and wash their hands;
  they quietly state the final terms for peace.
If they would let me know you as a man
  it would suffice.

UNFULFILLED

Man in fury
to fulfill
yawning love
builds infinity
of trodden moments
that refused
to be eternity

can't

stacks the cupboard of his heart
with wounded empty-bottle people
writhes hooked in dereliction
fast on the narcosis of a dream
the ecstasy of fresh surrender
always nothing long
feeling beauty growing ugly daily

WE SPIT

We spit upon God's face
each day
in myriad ways
though sometimes
his cries of pain
barely
reach our ears

who can bear
impassively
the false silence
of this muted world
when every howl of agony
behind locked doors
or dungeon walls
and every sigh
of lonely hopeless isolated
or intensely
tortured people
though blanketed by distance
screams
infinitely amplified
within the ears of God
and makes him almost stop
— through mercy —
here and now
the whole affair of being

BUTTERFLY

am I just a
pub-crawling butterfly
pollen-sozzled in the dazzle world
of infinite transient flowerdom
flitting in poiseworthy
playful mastery
with eyes for wings
sometimes glad of sunlight
swooping with crescendo silence
nectaring my days away
and leaving in my wake
a litany of colors
unconcerned for time
blending a blinding
eye-transcendent wing-speed
with careless summer doziness
about direction
who can dream me a
being more all round
infinite in beauty
than this drunk with joy
utterance of God
revelling in its finite
casual glory
caught by sunlight fluttering
on the storm's brink
almost conscious that each moment
is eternal
and seeming to be almost proud
of being no more tomorrow

WARSHOCK

on looking at a picture in the Pentagon

wide eyes
stare
out of nobody
into nothing

shell burst
mind burst
blind

like surf
men break
endlessly
on this beach

rippling the sand

GREY STONE IS MUSIC TO MY SILENCE

Grey stone is music to my silence.
Grey water takes the glamour from
the quiet sky.
I cannot feel at ease with beauty
while I know
that only distance and distraction
shield me from the agony
of men who now,
ambushed by famine or by anger,
fight with fear and have no chance to find
the satisfaction of the painted calm
that sunlight leaves us.

While men are striving brutally for food
how may I sit like this and watch the shadows
fall longer into the bird-stroked waters
where boats and oars wait carelessly and take
a noon siesta?
How can I fail to share
my brothers' blood-wrenched cry
against the ripping off of human life
for the proud glory of other men
who wish only
others to die?

Perhaps this pause can press more deeply
into my consciousness
the thorn that is my guilt:
my disregard of those for whom I care,

to whom I claim a closeness, whom I keep
far for my comfort.
Again — against my body's greed —
(or is this just excuse?)
this moment cries that for mankind
silence is urgent for replanting peace
and — that the plant succeed —
stillness is also need.

CRY AGONY

Cry agony at the infamy
of torn logic — reason's nerves,
pinnacle of man's perfection,
lying savaged by our crude incompetence
or rude impotence at tight thinking —
men called by Christ daring to call
all men brothers turn and first apply
After Shave then having wined and dined
watch in colour and with mild concern
— but no rage —
men cattled in the filth of sheds
or hungered in the dry air
hammered by sunlight
without food without friends without hope
without God
— brothers —
fast becoming bones.

MIST TOO CAN BE MEMORABLE

Mist too can be memorable
drifting at daybreak or at noon
over quiet water
or under the eave of reaching oaks
that tower above and stretch imperious
above the seaweed while the leaves waver
and the waves wait

tides remain our timepiece
steadily changing with their ebb and flow
— the tragicomedy
of human history —
heaving up or swallowing
the debris of the years

we wait
for ecstasy or suffering
to pass —
we watch
winter stillness break to movement
dance a while in warmth upon a branch
and fall golden
into the shadows

we hear
gulls that sing and squabble for their food
without thanksgiving
(moaning across the water or poised on garbage)
to an unknown God —

we know
moods that knive us raw apart
words that scalpel
and moments of oneness
too deep for sound
suffered in silence

we have watched and listened
and have heard
beyond the mist that drifts
over the quiet water
the wind swaying in the leaves above the sea
that it is good to be

IT'S SNOWING SILENCE OUT OF NOWHERE NOW

and the Silence was made flake
and drifted upon us . . .

It's snowing Silence out of nowhere now
and no one seems to know quite what this means,
unless it means that words have had their day
and Silence is now master of all things.
Perhaps the words that should have brought us close
have shouted us apart right at the seams,
so Silence settles on the human heart
and drifts down out of nowhere on flake wings.
The flakes that gesture white against the door
conduct a silent requiem for war.

PEOPLE TELL ME

People tell me "Don't be afraid of God,
for God is Love."
O don't you see
I fear the very Lover
in my God!

I fear the Lover
hiding glory in the drab disguise
of humble people

I fear the Lover
barely daring to reveal
his gentle breeze of being
lest majesty beget
tremendous homage

I fear the one who loves me
and touches with such tenderness
this fragile thing of freedom that is "me"
lest it be shattered

and yet perhaps I have no fear of God
but of his being Love
and so of me

I fear the fact that he is Love and so
must leave me all the drama of decision
that love requires
                 — as sure as light reveals

and darkness veils, I too must choose
the narrow way, the holocaust, the bleak
leap of abandonment into the barely known
and yet demanding deep —
I fear the fact that I am made to choose
and so may lose

FEBRUARY DAWN

There is a whole landscape this morning
frozen on the inside of the windows
a sweeping mountain slope of ice
topped with individual blades of trees
— mostly pine —
each with its own perfect crystal branches
a whole mountain blown by winter air
in Steuben glass with casual precision
and out beyond the landscape now the sun
gilds the water tower that through the night
has watched the town and waited for the dawn
some fine white smoke moves like mist
against the apple sky
everything else is still

TWO FOOLS

two tumble in space
but only one
knows the comedy
of being wrong

one fool
with a foot on the moon
forgets the hands
at the Potter's wheel

one knows
the Clown Creator
shaping clay
into laughter

two tumble in space
but only one
knows that tragedy
will be gone

DISTILLED IN THE SLOW DARKNESS

learning to live with patience and abide
calm and unhurried the full brunt of time
moving with daylight shadows into the past
biding the chosen moment —
savouring gladly the season of events
swung slow or swift across the mind's wide screen
happy with movement and at rest alive
tasting the firelight fullness ambered deep
blazing a quiet gold within the glass
distilled in the slow darkness of the years
without panic perfect into being

MESSIAH

anoint the wounds
of my spirit
with the balm
of forgiveness
pour the oil
of your calm
on the waters
of my heart

take the squeal
of frustration
from the wheels
of my passion
that the power
of your tenderness
may smooth
the way I love

that the tedium
of giving
in the risk
of surrender
and the reaching
out naked
to a world
that must wound

may be kindled
fresh daily
to a blaze

of compassion
that the grain
may fall gladly
to burst in the ground
— and the harvest abound.

BEING OLDER

being older
is being conscious
of being bones

posing the question
as right and proper
of the dust doorway
with the skull knocker

daring to plunge
in thoughts of void
or kingdom come

being older
is tasting life
with a new tongue

knowing the sap
will fail to run

seeing new
touching new
loving new

and being bolder
for being bones

THE EVE OF FALLING

like leaves more glorious on the eve of falling
    caught radiant in October light
or swallows flexing for the long migration
    valued now for their impending flight
so now your face your eyes your laughter
    I watch with a wonder touched with sorrow
knowing that my God in you
    — this blaze — will not be here tomorrow

CLOUDS

Everything is breathtaking, but clouds
reveal the Master Artist and provide
a Sistine Chapel ceiling for the world;
towering up in foam against the blue
in billow upon billow, cotton-white,
they soar with majesty in slow magnificence
and mood the watcher as he sees the night
of thunder nearing.

Sometimes he plays the spectrum of his palette
and handles color as Bach handled sound,
playing at evening in some village church
a fugue through the open doors and out
into the Swiss mountains.

God handles color as Bach handled sound
and in the ripples of each dusk or dawn
he shows a casual mastery in patient blood
— purple, crimson, red or liquid gold —
greater than the mushroom cloud of man's
massive impotence.

LIFE IS SIMPLER TOWARDS EVENING

life is simpler towards evening
shadows longer quieter
and more complete
things are calm

we no longer throttle speech
from mystery
but having lived through long years
respect silence

we no longer audit God's accounts
with the same agony
but knowing him more deeply know that he
is good for loving

now vision comes
only in lightning
leaving us blinder than before
but more aware
that change remains our permanent despair

pulled by a current out of our control
we live in a growing past
the myth of happiness stains our empty glass
time corks the joy of every swift delight
but moments test the passing wine
and find in it a tang of the eternal

FAILED SPECIES?

For twenty million years or more
This planet fed the Dinosaur.
It makes you sit a while and think
How soon young Man may be extinct.
But though he turn this chip of star
To ash touched from some fine cigar
When all the galaxies are dark
Man still will reign who shares God's heart.